E Correct the eight words that are spelled incorrectly.

I ~~recomend~~ studying at ~~universitie~~ in Great Britain.
~~You're~~ English will be ~~excelent~~ and I'm ~~shore~~ ~~yule~~ be
sucesfull.

recommend _____ _____

_____ _____ _____

_____ _____

F True (✔) or false(✗)?

1 A cushion on a bed is called a pill.   ✗ *It is called a pillow.*

2 A school where children live and sleep is called a
boring school.   _____

3 If you go driving during the rush hour, you'll
probably find yourself stuck in a traffic jam.   _____

4 Housework is work that is given by teachers for
students to do at home.   _____

5 'I needn't have gone to the hospital' means the same
as 'I didn't need to go to the hospital.'   _____

G Write the words with a similar meaning on the same line:

chubby   dreadful   clever   gorgeous
bright   handsome   ~~awful~~   overweight

bad   *awful*   , _____

beautiful   _____ , _____

fat   _____ , _____

intelligent   _____ , _____

H What is this?

1 back to front
2 inside out
3 upside down ⟋
4 straight away

I Which is the odd one out (= which word is different)? If you
need help, look at the Colour pages at the back of the dictionary.

1 wok   <u>stew</u>   steamer   chip pan
*You use a wok, steamer and chip pan to cook food. A stew
is a type of food.*

2 glider   hovercraft   liner   yacht

3 basil   cloves   mint   parsley

4 briefcase   rucksack   shoulder bag   trainers

5 barn   busker   orchard   stable

Photocopiable © Oxford University Press

Getting things right

Where can I find the information to help me?

Wordpower can help you in many different ways. Remember to look in all the possible places that could help you.

Which tense should I use?
▸ Information about grammar, including tenses, the passive, nouns and relative clauses, is in the Grammar section at the back of the dictionary.

Which preposition?
▸ You can find information about prepositions at the entry for the word.

It's a phrasal verb but which particle do I need?
▸ Look at the section marked **PHR V** at the entry for the verb.

Do I need a gerund or an infinitive?
▸ Look at Verb patterns. It will tell you about many of the most common ones.

I think I know which word it is but I'm not sure.
▸ Hundreds of usage notes explain the differences between similar words.

Is it an irregular verb?
▸ Check the list at the back of the dictionary.

Is it an idiom?
▸ Check in the section marked **IDM** at the entry for one of the main words in it.

Don't forget to look at the example sentences, which will show you the most common patterns and collocations of a word.

Fill in the missing words

Complete the following text by writing the correct word or words in each space. The notes above will help you to use your dictionary to find the answers.

Measuring up to 10 feet at the shoulder and ¹_____ up to 12 000 lbs, the African elephant is the heaviest land mammal. It keeps cool by covering itself ²_____ mud or dust, which also helps protect it ³_____ the sun and ⁴_____ insects. Numbers have reduced drastically as elephants ⁵_____ killed for their ivory. This is now illegal, but still goes ⁶_____ . Some are also killed ⁷_____ farmers, who face the impossible job of keeping elephants ⁸_____ their crops. Their tusks are actually two teeth. They are

different sizes and shapes depending ⁹_____ where the elephant lives and what jobs the elephant uses them for. They can be used ¹⁰_____ digging, fighting, lifting or removing obstacles. Female elephants and young males live ¹¹_____ family groups. Typically, a family group consists ¹²_____ a mother and her daughters and grandchildren. Males leave the herd when they ¹³_____ adults and live ¹⁴_____ or in other groups of males.

Photocopiable © Oxford University Press

s do not
rite in book #

Oxford
Wordpower
Trainer

Contents

Key to exercises at
www.oup.com/elt/teacher/wordpower

Quick quiz

Learn how to use Wordpower by doing this quick quiz.
You can find all the answers in the dictionary.

A Circle the correct word.

1 I don't feel very well – I think I've got a stomach bee / (bug) / insect / worm.

2 I'm having a do / a laugh / a make / a play to celebrate my birthday.

3 A walrus / A stag / A hedgehog / An elephant is a large animal that has a trunk and two tusks.

4 Could I make / have / do / see a look at your new dictionary, please?

5 I didn't understand the word, so I looked it away / down / out / up in my dictionary.

B Cross out the wrong words.

I asked the teacher ~~help~~ / to help / ~~helping~~ me, but she told me / ~~told to me~~ that I should ~~make~~ / do more homework, learn ~~use~~ / ~~using~~ / to use my dictionary, and ~~give~~ / pay attention to / ~~with~~ / ~~of~~ her in class.

C Match the words which rhyme (= have the same sound).

height	half
laugh	kite
queue	rough
sew	though
stuff	zoo

D Match the British and American English words.

dressing gown	vest
nappy	sneakers
trainers	pants
trousers	diaper
waistcoat	bathrobe

Photocopiable © Oxford University Press

Spot the error

In each line of the text there is one mistake. <u>Underline</u> the mistake and write the correct word at the end of the line.

The owner of a house in Leeds could not <u>beleive</u> his eyes when   _believe_
he returned from work to find a cold and embarassed burglar   _____
laying in his garden. While trying to cut through the wires   _____
of the burglar alarm, he <u>did</u> a mistake and instead cut a main   _____
electric cable. Incredibly, he <u>recieved</u> only minor burns and   _____
cuts. The owner of the flat said, 'I was amazed for how calm he   _____
was when I found him. If he <u>has</u> fallen onto the concrete path,   _____
he would have been gravely hurt or even killed, but he <u>felt</u> into   _____
bushes.' The lucky burglar thanked the man for saving his life: _____
'He stopped me to freeze to death,' he said, 'and because of   _____
him, I've decided retire from crime.'   _____

Sentence transformations

Use the word given in **bold** to complete the second sentence so that it has a similar meaning to the first sentence. For help with this exercise, look at the entry for the given word in the dictionary, or look at the Grammar section at the back.

▸ *Example*: 'Can you tell me how to get to the city centre?' she asked me. (directions)
    She asked me _for directions/to give her directions_ to the city centre.

1 I'm off to the shop because we've drunk nearly all the milk. (**running**)
   I'm off to the shop because _____
   _____ milk.

2 We're considering buying a new car. (**thinking**)
   We're _____ buying a new car.

3 I really had a good time in Australia. (**enjoyed**)
   I really _____ in Australia.

4 'Let's all go out and celebrate tonight,' James said. (**suggested**)
   James _____ that night.

5 Police are questioning a man in connection with the robbery. (**questioned**)
   A man _____ in connection with the robbery.

6 It's possible that he didn't get my message. (**might**)
   He _____ my message.

7 There's almost no money left in our account. (**hardly**)
   There's _____ left in our account.

8 The party was so boring that we left early. (**such**)
   It was _____ that we left early.

9 I can't wait to meet her new boyfriend. (**dying**)
   I'm _____ her new boyfriend.

10 I arrived late, so I missed the train. (**earlier**)
    If I _____ caught the train.

Photocopiable © Oxford University Press

Verb patterns

Gap fills

Fill the gaps with the correct form of the verb.

1 She denied _stealing_ the purse.
   steal

2 I tried to stop the man _____ the dog. hit

3 The dog has learnt _____ the door. open

4 I can't stand _____ animals in pain. see

5 I've arranged _____ him tomorrow. meet

6 I attempted _____ in French. speak

7 I'll never forget _____ him for the first time. meet

8 My dad discouraged me from _____ the army. join

9 I really enjoy _____ crosswords. do

10 He apologized for _____ late. be

Sentence transformations

Using the word given, complete the second sentence so that it has a similar meaning to the first sentence. You must use between two and five words, including the word given. If you need help, look up the bold word in the dictionary.

1 I can't wait to see you again.
   looking
   I'm _looking forward to seeing_ you again.

2 Did your parents allow you to go out at night? let
   Did your parents _____ out at night?

3 I wish I hadn't told her my secret.
   regret
   I _____ my secret.

4 I'll always remember the first time I saw her. forget
   I'll _____ for the first time.

5 Why don't you talk to your parents about the problem? try
   You ought to _____ about the problem.

6 Pregnant woman should not drink alcohol. avoid
   Pregnant women should _____

7 I can't buy the tickets until he tells me if he wants one. waiting
   I'm _____ me if he wants a ticket.

8 I recommend you do more exercise.
   advise
   I _____ more exercise.

9 The salesman talked her into buying the car. persuaded
   The salesman _____ the car.

10 He managed to get a place at university. succeeded
   He _____ a place at university.

Verb forms

Many regular verbs change their spelling in the 3rd person singular present, the present participle, the past and the past participle forms. For example, **hurry**:

▸ *She hurries   She is hurry**ing***
  *She hurr**ied** / has hurr**ied***

In the Wordpower dictionary, irregular spellings are shown beside the headword in each entry.

Complete the statements below with the correct form of the verb in brackets.

1 I _____ (study) French
   when I was at university.

2 Last year I went _____ (ski)
   on holiday.

3 I really like _____ (shop) for
   clothes.

4 I go _____ (swim) every
   week.

5 I have never _____ (panic)
   before a test or an exam.

Countable, uncountable and plural nouns

Cross out the wrong form. If you need help, look up the **bold** words and read the GRAMMAR notes.

1 Could I borrow a scissors/a pair of
   scissors?

2 I'd like some **information/
   informations** about bus tours,
   please.

3 The **pasta** aren't/isn't cooked yet.

4 How many **homeworks**/much
   homework did your teacher give you?

5 His job is restoring antique
   furniture/furnitures.

6 I had two **toasts**/pieces of **toast** for
   breakfast.

7 My **accommodation** was/were very
   basic.

8 He gave us lots of **advice/advices**.

9 I never read newspapers because the
   news is/are so depressing.

10 This **trouser**/These **trousers** is/are too
    small for me.

Collocations

Fill the gaps with a word from the list below. You can find all the answers by looking at example sentences in Wordpower.

How to succeed in sport!

If you enjoy ¹_____ sport, why
not try ²_____ in a competition?
Of course, you will have to ³_____
hard. You also need to be in good
⁴_____ and have a lot of
⁵_____ . If you are good enough,
you might even win a ⁶_____ !
Don't worry if you ⁷_____ ,
because you may ⁸_____ next
time. Who knows, one day you might
⁹_____ the world record or
become the world ¹⁰_____ !

1 making	6 reward
to play	prize
doing	respect
to do	price
2 entering	7 defeat
joining	beat
going	lose
taking part	miss
3 rehearse	8 gain
train	pass
coach	beat
audition	win
4 fit	9 pass
strength	master
stamina	break
shape	exceed
5 stamina	10 master
health	champion
fitness	leader
exercise	amateur

Phrasal verbs

Which particle?

What does the particle back mean in these sentences?

I'll call you back later.
She wrote to him but he didn't write back.

Many particles keep their meaning, even when used with different verbs:

▸ Go on. I want to know what happens next!

▸ They liked the hotel so much that they stayed on for an extra week.

▸ When I picked up the mug the handle came off.

▸ I didn't pay the bill and now my phone's been cut off.

A Match the particles with their meanings.

back	separate, no longer attached
on	in return
off	continuing

B Fill in the missing particle (back, on, or off) in these sentences.

1 I lent that book to George last week, but he hasn't given it _____ yet.

2 The police have sealed _____ the street where the attack took place.

3 When you've finished with the book please pass it _____ to the next student.

4 Louis got into trouble for answering his teacher _____ when she told him off in class.

5 Although it was very late we decided to push _____ to the next village.

6 The road branches _____ to the left a little way up ahead.

More particles

Fill the blanks with the correct particle.

1 Business is pretty bad these days. A lot of workers have been laid

_____ .

(over, off, down)

2 "U.S." stands _____ United States.
(out, to, for)

3 I can't figure _____ how to use this gadget.
(up, out, for)

4 Sue came _____ the letter while she was cleaning her room.
(to, across, for)

5 I'm sure that story wasn't true. I think Pete made it _____ .
(up, for, in)

6 She was offered a job in Dallas, but she decided to turn it _____ .
(over, up, down)

7 Alex dropped out _____ school when he was 16 years old.
(for, of, from)

8 Please write _____ your address and phone number.
(down, over, away)

Photocopiable © Oxford University Press

Separable and inseparable verbs

Fill in the blanks by putting the word 'it' in the correct place.
In each sentence you will have to leave one blank empty.

1 You must be hot with your coat on. Why don't you take
   _it_ off ___ ?

2 If you don't understand this word, look ___ up ___ in
   your dictionary.

3 He had a very bad illness, and it will take him a long
   time to get ___ over ___ .

4 I was going to do my homework last night, but I didn't
   get around ___ to ___ .

5 I thought you had finished reading the newspaper, so I
   threw ___ away ___ .

6 Jill can't come to the meeting tomorrow, so we'll have
   to put ___ off ___ until next week.

Opposites

Many phrasal verbs have opposites. You will learn them
more quickly if you memorize them together.

Match each sentence in 1-10 with its opposite in a-j.
Then write the pairs of opposites in the spaces below.

1 It was getting dark so I turned on the light.

2 Don't leave your bag on the floor like that – pick it up!

3 It's cold – put your coat on.

4 I bought Jon a present to cheer him up.

5 You should check in at reception as soon as you arrive.

6 I pulled over at the side of the road to look at the map.

7 I tried to learn the guitar but packed it in after a few weeks.

8 My dad is coming to pick me up at ten.

9 A 10% service charge is added on to the bill.

10 I'm so tired. I can't wait to get home and sit down.

a I can drop you off on my way home if you like.

b You have to check out of the hotel before midday.

c Take off that silly hat!

d I've decided to take up aerobics.

e Did you see that? That driver pulled out right in front of me.

f Don't forget to turn off the TV before you go to bed.

g We all stood up when the head teacher came into the classroom.

h What's thirty-one take away fourteen?

i He put the book down on the table.

j Don't let the exams get you down.

turn sth on _turn sth off_   add sth on ___   pick sb up ___
put sth on ___   pick sth up ___   sit down ___
check in ___   cheer sb up ___
pack sth in ___   pull over ___

Photocopiable © Oxford University Press

Idioms

An idiom is a particular combination of words, which has a special meaning that is difficult to guess, even if you know the meanings of the individual words in it. To find an idiom in Wordpower, look up the most important word in it (ignoring words like 'off' and 'the'). You will find the idiom in the idioms section, marked **IDM**. For example, to find **by heart**, look at **heart**.

A Match the sentences to the pictures and then fill in the blanks with the parts of the body from the list. Use each word only once.

eye eyes nose ~~chest~~ head head back mind heart arm heels feet

1 Doctor, there's something I need to **get off** my _chest_. [d]

2 I don't know what's wrong with the boss today. I only asked a question and she **bit** my _____ **off!** [ ]

3 We weren't really arguing until Basil came along and **stuck** his _____ **in**. [ ]

4 I can't possibly meet you today. I'm **up to** my _____ in work at the moment. [ ]

5 As she walked up the aisle towards Tom, Sue started to **get cold** _____. [ ]

6 When John left me for another woman, he **broke** my _____. [ ]

7 I have to sit near the water's edge so I can **keep an** _____ **on** Emma. [ ]

8 Oh all right, I'll come and watch it with you. You've **twisted** my _____. [ ]

9 I fell _____ **over** _____ **in love** with her the moment I saw her, but she doesn't want to know me. [ ]

10 As I walked away, I could hear them whispering about me **behind** my _____. [ ]

11 He was in the shop for ages trying to **make up** his _____ what to buy. [ ]

B Replace the word or phrase in bold in sentences 1–10 with one of the idioms shown in the pictures opposite, changing verb forms, pronouns, etc. as necessary.

▸ It would make me very sad *if anything happened to my cat.*

▸ It **would break my heart** *if anything happened to my cat.*

1 Could you **watch** my bags for me while I go into the shop, please?

2 The way we bring up the children is our business. I don't want your mother **interfering!**

3 Mark and Emma are both still **crazy about each other** even after five years.

4 He was going to report it to the police, but at the last minute he **felt too scared** and decided to keep quiet.

5 Why not tell him how you feel? It might do you good to **talk about it.**

6 Fran says she's too busy to come to the party tonight. See if you can **persuade her.**

7 You'll just have to **decide** which one you want. I'm not waiting any longer!

8 When I asked him what he wanted to eat, he just **shouted at me.**

9 It's not fair of us to discuss Jo's work **without her knowing about it.**

10 We're so busy because we've just moved house and we **have got loads of boxes** that need unpacking.

Photocopiable © Oxford University Press

Confusable words

-ing or -ed adjectives

Some adjectives have an –ing form and an –ed form. Compare:

▸ *I hate doing the ironing. It's so boring!*
▸ *I'm bored. What shall we do?*

A Underline the correct adjective in each sentence.

1 People who talk about football all the time are bored/boring.

2 The scenery in the Swiss Alps is absolutely amazed/amazing.

3 When Ann realized what a fool she'd made of herself, she felt terribly embarrassed/embarrassing.

4 Don't go to that restaurant – the food is revolted/revolting.

5 The film was so moved/moving that I cried at the end.

6 Looking after children all day long is very tired/tiring. By the evening, I'm completely exhausting/exhausted.

7 I couldn't put this book down. It's really excited/exciting!

8 She is terrified/terrifying of spiders.

B Are the adjectives in the correct form? Mark any that are correct with a tick (✔) and any that are wrong with a cross (✘).

1 That boy is really annoyed. I wish he would go away! ✘ *annoying*

2 She's a charmed woman and she tells fascinating stories.

3 After a relaxing bath, she felt refreshing.

4 The theme park was disappointed. Most of the rides were really boring. There was only one ride which the children thought was frightened.

5 My job is challenging and I generally enjoy it, but it has its bored moments, too.

6 Some of the students' exam results were disappointed, but on the whole, I'm quite satisfying with their progress.

Using illustrations

You can see the difference between similar words by looking at the black and white illustrations in Wordpower.

Each of the words 1 – 10 is shown in an illustration. Find the illustration in the dictionary and choose the correct word a–d.

1 …it's what you do to make food and drink go down your throat to your stomach.
   a   bite
   b   lick
   c   sneeze
   d   swallow

2 …it's something you do when you want to get toothpaste out of a tube.
   a   crush
   b   squash
   c   press
   d   squeeze

3 …it's a tool with a heavy metal head that you use for hitting nails, etc.
   a   a chisel
   b   a drill
   c   a hammer
   d   a mallet

4 …it's when you sit on the floor with your legs pulled up in front of you and with one leg or foot over the other.
   a   back to front
   b   cross-legged
   c   inside out
   d   with your legs crossed

Photocopiable © Oxford University Press

5 ...it's a large shellfish with eight legs. It is bluish-black but it turns red when it is cooked.
   a   a clam
   b   a lobster
   c   a mussel
   d   an oyster

6 ...it's a type of kitchen tool that has a metal or plastic net, used for separating solids from liquids or very small pieces of food from large pieces.
   a   a colander
   b   a grater
   c   a ladle
   d   a sieve

7 ...it's what a stone or rock does when you throw it into water.
   a   float
   b   ripple
   c   sink
   d   bounce

8 ...it's a row of bushes or trees planted close together at the edge of a garden or field to separate one piece of land from another.
   a   a fence
   b   a gate
   c   a hedge
   d   a wall

9 ...it's when you allow somebody to use something for a short time, or give somebody money that must be paid back.
   a   afford
   b   borrow
   c   lend
   d   owe

10 ...it's what a ball does when you throw it onto a hard surface.
   a   bounce
   b   hop
   c   jump
   d   smash

Write the correct word

Complete the following sentences by choosing the correct verb from each pair in **bold**. Remember to put the verbs into the appropriate tense.

1 My father ___taught___ me to drive when I was 17. (teach/learn)

2 I got in the taxi and asked the driver to _____ me to the airport. (bring/take)

3 Hurry up or we'll _____ the bus! (miss/lose)

4 She's only in her forties, but with her grey hair, she _____ seventy. (seem/look)

5 Several buildings were badly _____ in the blast, but luckily no one was _____ . (damage/hurt)

6 Guess what? My wife _____ a baby! (expect/wait)

7 When you come to class tomorrow, _____ your dictionaries. (bring/take)

Bring the newspaper

Fetch the newspaper

Take the newspaper

Confusable words

8 _____ bald is a sure sign that you are _____ old. (get/go)

9 Don't _____ time queuing to go up the tower. The view from the top isn't worth it. (waste/lose)

10 The price of oil _____ dramatically at the moment. (rise/raise)

11 From what I could hear, the couple _____ to be having an argument about money. (seem/look)

12 I _____ in the east of the country and moved west in my early twenties. (grow/grow up)

13 The prisoner _____ escape by digging a tunnel. (can/manage to)

14 If I had a good job, I'd _____ lots of money. (earn/win)

15 We _____ each other at university. (know/get to know)

What's the difference?

Cross out the wrong word(s).

1 Our trip to London was ~~funny~~/fun. (funny = that makes you laugh/ fun = enjoyable)

2 We had a great landscape/scenery/ view from our hotel window.

3 The doctor gave me a receipt/recipe/ prescription for some antibiotics.

4 You shouldn't take what he says seriously. You're just too sensitive/sensible.

5 She works like/as a receptionist in a big hotel.

6 I lived there during/since/for ten years and came back to the UK five years since/ago/for.

7 She has a good job/work in Brussels.

8 The band are actually/currently touring in the US and won't be back until early autumn.

9 She lives on her own and says she never gets alone/lonely.

10 John will pass the exam because he's worked very hard/hardly.

Collocation – Words that go together

Expressions with *make*, *do*, *give*, *have* and *take*

The only way to learn collocations is to collect them and keep practising them, but there are just a few points that can help you decide which verb to use:

Do is often used for tasks and duties that you have to do and that are not creative, or in expressions with the words thing, nothing, anything, etc.:

▸ do the cleaning
▸ do an exam
▸ do a job
▸ do something wrong
▸ do things your own way
▸ nothing to do

Make is often used when sth is produced by you, using your skills, your mind or your words:

- ▸ make dinner
- ▸ make a movie
- ▸ make a model
  (**But** do a painting)
- ▸ make a decision
- ▸ make a judgement
- ▸ make a guess
- ▸ make a comment
- ▸ make an excuse
- ▸ make a suggestion
- ▸ make a promise

Give, too, is used in many expressions connected with words. It is also used in expressions that describe physical actions:

- ▸ give (sb) advice
- ▸ give (sb) your word
- ▸ give a reason
- ▸ give a lecture
- ▸ give evidence
- ▸ give sth a kick/a twist/a push
- ▸ give sb a slap/a kiss/a hug

Complete each of the following sentences with the verb make, do, give, have or take:

1 He couldn't _____ a good explanation why he was late.

2 Are you _____ anything next Sunday?

3 Did anyone _____ a comment about the food?

4 We are going to have some difficult choices to _____ .

5 You should _____ some stretching before you run.

6 I think Barry's _____ an argument with his mother.

7 My brother doesn't like _____ risks.

8 He _____ his friend a friendly punch on the arm.

9 Shall we _____ a five-minute break?

10 I _____ a short cut through the woods.

11 Are you _____ a party on your birthday?

12 She _____ her word that she'd keep my secret.

13 I always _____ a lot of photos on holiday.

14 I told him to slow down but he _____ no notice.

15 Have you _____ any plans for next year?

16 I'll _____ you a call later.

17 I'm just going to _____ a phone call.

18 You can _____ a lot of money working with computers.

19 Those boys have just come here to _____ trouble.

20 People kept _____ jokes about her hair.

Word formation

Long words are often made from shorter words with a few letters added to the beginning (a prefix) or to the end (a suffix). These pages show you some important groups of prefixes and suffixes. There is a longer alphabetical list at the back of Wordpower which will help you with the quiz questions.

Prefixes

Numbers

A word that begins with bi- shows that there are two of something. A *bicycle* has two wheels (but a *tricycle* has three). Words for metric measurements are often made with the prefixes cent-, kilo-, etc. 100 *centimetres* = 1 metre, 1 *kilogram* = 1,000 grams, and so on.

1 How many sides does an octagon have?
2 If 1976 was the bicentennial of Mozart's death, in which year did he die?
3 Which word is a monosyllable, 'but', 'although', or 'however'?
4 Does a multinational company exist in only one country?

Time

A number of prefixes are connected with time, for example pre- (before) and ex- (former). A *prearranged* meeting was arranged beforehand. A divorced man might talk about his *ex-wife*. The *ex-president* is no longer president.

5 If a house was built in the postwar period, was it built before or after the war?
6 If a baby is premature, is it born before or after the expected time?

Size and degree

Some common prefixes tell us 'how big' or 'how much'. A word that begins with maxi- is large or the greatest; mini- refers to something small (*miniskirt*). extra- means 'more' – *extra-strong glue* is stronger than usual.

7 Which is bigger, a store or a superstore?
8 If something is microscopic, is it very large or very small?
9 How do you feel if you have overeaten – very full or still hungry?

Negative

Many prefixes change the meaning of a word to its opposite or make it negative. A *nonsmoker* does not smoke; the opposite of happy is *unhappy*. We also use in- (or before certain letters im-, il-, or ir-) in this way.

10 Which of the prefixes un-, in-, im-, il-, ir- would you use to make the opposites of these words?
   correct   certain   possible   regular
   sure   legal   valid   relevant
   patient   legible

Position

These prefixes tell us where something is or happens. For example, sub- gives the idea of 'under': a *subway* goes under the road; we read the *subtitles* under the pictures of a foreign movie.

11 Is an activity that is extra-curricular part of the curriculum of a school?
12 Is a flight from New York to London transatlantic?

Photocopiable © Oxford University Press

Suffixes

A suffix is added to the end of a word, and it often changes the function of the word. For example, -ly makes an adjective into an adverb. (*He sings beautifully. The car was badly damaged.*)

To make nouns that describe a state, an action or a quality you can add a suffix such as -ation. e.g. *inform + ation = information*; *examine + ation = examination*. There may be small changes in the spelling, e.g. the second 'e' is dropped in *examination*.

Other suffixes are used to make nouns that describe people, for example, -er, -or, -ist, -ian, -ee, -ant, -ent. They may be added to a verb to describe the person who does the action, e.g. *rider*, *sailor*, *cyclist*, or we can add them to nouns to describe someone who works on a particular subject (*artist*, *historian*).

We can also make a noun or an adjective into a verb by adding a suffix such as -en, -ify or -ize. If we make something wider, simpler or more modern, we *widen*, *simplify* or *modernize* it.

13 Use one of the suffixes -ation, -ment, -ness to make nouns from these verbs and adjectives:
develop   kind   arrange
imagine   happy   organize
What happens to the spelling of 'happy'?

14 Fill the gaps to make words that describe people and their jobs:
a ____ or   (works in a theatre)
t ____ er   (works in a school)
c _____ or (stands in front of an orchestra)
e _____ er (goes out to discover new countries)

15 Which verbs can you make from these words, using one of the suffixes -ize, -en and -ify?
summary   false   sharp
general   loose   pure
(You may need to change the spelling a little.)

Prefixes and Suffixes

Using the prefixes and suffixes below, change the words in bold to complete the sentences.

-ally -ment -ify extra- trans- -ous -ward -able il- -ish

1 Simpler language would make this report more _____ . read

2 What do people in your country _____ eat at Christmas? tradition

3 Have you got this shirt in an _____? This one's not big enough. large

4 When I mixed all the paints together I got a _____ colour. brown

5 It's _____ to sell cigarettes to children under 16. legal

6 I think you should _____ these instructions – they're too complicated. simple

7 Passing your driving test first time was quite an _____ . achieve

8 When is the next _____ flight from London to Boston? Atlantic

9 Don't eat those berries – they're _____ . poison

10 Travel _____ for about eight miles until you reach a junction. north

Photocopiable © Oxford University Press

Prepositions

Prepositions of place

Fill each gap with one of the prepositions shown below.

1 It took us ages to get there, because we had to drive for two miles _____ a tractor.

2 Where's my dictionary? I left it _____ the table.

3 Can you get the ice cream? It's _____ the freezer.

4 They live on the top floor, in the flat _____ mine.

5 She spends all day sitting _____ a computer.

6 The cinema is _____ the bank.

7 Philadelphia is situated _____ New York and Washington DC.

8 He placed a ladder _____ the side of the house.

The bird is in/ inside the cage.

The lamp is above the table.

The meat is on the table.

The cat is under the table.

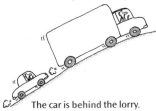

The lorry is in front of the car.

The car is behind the lorry.

Sam is between Kim and Tom.

The temperature is below zero.

Kim is next to / beside Sam.

Tom is opposite Kim.

The house is among the trees.

The girl is leaning against the wall.

Photocopiable © Oxford University Press

Prepositions of time

in

parts of the day (not night)		*in the morning(s),*
		in the evening(s), etc.
	months	*in February*
	seasons	*in (the) summer*
	years	*in 1995*
	decades	*in the 1920's*
	centuries	*in the 20th century*
	after some time	*in a moment*
		in ten minutes

at

clock time	*at 5 o'clock*
	at 7.45 p.m.
night	*at night*
holiday periods	*at Christmas*
	at the weekend
now	*at the moment*
	at present

on

day of the week	*on Saturdays*
	on Friday morning
dates	*on (the) 20th (of) May*
	(US also on May 20th)
particular days	*on Christmas Day*
	on New Year's Day
	on Good Friday
	on my birthday
	on the following day

Write the word or phrase in the appropriate column.

2010
29th May
6 o'clock
9 a.m.
afternoon
Easter
last year
lunchtime
March
New Year's Eve
next month
night
spring
the 1980's
the 21st century
the day after tomorrow
the weekend
today
tomorrow
Tuesday
Wednesday morning
yesterday

in	at	on	no preposition
2010			

Do you find it difficult to learn prepositions? Look at
Learning vocabulary in Wordpower for some useful ideas!

Photocopiable © Oxford University Press

Prepositions ☑

Letter writing

Informal letter

You have just received this letter from your friend and made some notes on it. Write a suitable reply, using all the information in your notes.

Write a letter of between 120 and 180 words in an appropriate style.

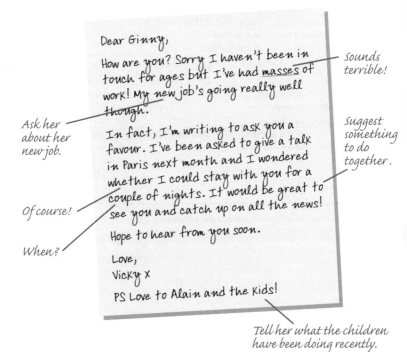

Dear Ginny,

How are you? Sorry I haven't been in touch for ages but I've had masses of work! My new job's going really well though.

Sounds terrible!

Ask her about her new job.

In fact, I'm writing to ask you a favour. I've been asked to give a talk in Paris next month and I wondered whether I could stay with you for a couple of nights. It would be great to see you and catch up on all the news!

Suggest something to do together.

Of course!

Hope to hear from you soon.

When?

Love,
Vicky X

PS Love to Alain and the kids!

Tell her what the children have been doing recently.

Job application letter

Job application letters usually have four paragraphs:
1 Where you saw the job advertisement + why you are writing
2 Your skills and experience
3 Why you would like the job
4 When you will be available + an appropriate ending to the letter

Look at the phrases below. Which paragraph should they be in? Write a number from 1-4. The first two are done for you.

- As you will see from my CV, _2_
- Further to your advertisement in "English World", _1_
- I am a qualified and experienced teacher, translator, etc. ___
- I am currently working … ___
- I am keen/eager to find a position as a … ___
- I have a great deal of experience of …ing … ___
- I look forward to hearing from you (soon). ___

Photocopiable © Oxford University Press

Writing a reply

Here is one possible reply to the letter on the previous page.
Fill the gaps in the letter with a word or phrase from the list.

wonderful news

Do you fancy

It was great to
hear from you

exactly

Hi

please write
soon

sounds

I wish

well worth

let me know

spend much
time

_____ Vicky!

Thanks for your letter. _____ . I can't
believe you're coming to Paris – that's _____
_____ ! Of course you can stay at our place. You
know you're always welcome. When _____
are you coming?

Will you have any free time while you're here? It would
be nice to do some sightseeing. _____
going to the Palace of Versailles? It'll be packed with
tourists, but it's _____ visiting.

Your new job _____ terribly stressful. Are
your colleagues nice? Kevin and Sylvie are in their 4th
year at secondary school now, though they don't
_____ studying: he's out at parties every
weekend and she's busy with her rock band. Sometimes
_____ we'd never had twins!

Anyway, _____ and _____
what your plans are.

Take care,
Ginny

- I will be available from July 1st until
  August 30th. ___
- I would like to apply for the post
  of … ___
- I would love the chance/opportunity
  to … ___
- In my work as a … I have often had
  to … ___
- Last year I worked in …/as a … ___
- My responsibilities include …
  and … ___

- Please find attached a copy of my CV.
  (= for an email) ___
- Please find enclosed a copy of my CV.
  (= for a letter) ___
- This would be the ideal opportunity
  for me to … ___
- Yours faithfully, (= if you write Dear
  Sir/Madam) ___
- Yours sincerely, (= if you write Dear
  Mr/Ms Smith, etc.) ___

Essay writing

Linking expressions

A Fill each space with a linking expression. Use each expression only once.

Although	Furthermore	The first advantage
As a result	In addition to this	The main advantage
Consequently	In conclusion	There is a great deal of debate
Even though	Many people are talking	~~These days~~
For example	Moreover	To conclude
For instance	~~Nowadays~~	To sum up
For this reason	On the other hand	What is more

Introduction

1 a _Nowadays_____ there is a lot of traffic on the roads.
  b _These days_____

2 a _____ about the advantages and disadvantages of having a car.
  b _____

Advantages paragraph

3 a _____ of owning a car is the freedom that it gives you.
  b _____

4 a _____, it allows you to go wherever you like, whenever you like.
  b _____

5 a _____, you can carry passengers and luggage.
  b _____
  c _____
  d _____

Disadvantages paragraph

6 a _____ , owning a car does have disadvantages.

7 a _____ cars are useful, they also cause pollution.
  b _____

8 You have to pay for petrol and repairs, and pay tax and insurance.

  a _____ , owning a car can be very expensive.
  b _____
  c _____

Conclusion

9 a _____ , for many people, a car is an expensive luxury.
  b _____
  c _____

B Write each expression in the correct box below.

According to…	Furthermore	Secondly
Although	However	The majority believe
As a result	In addition	Therefore
Despite	In conclusion	~~These days~~
Firstly	In my opinion	To conclude
For this reason	Moreover	To sum up
From my point of view	On the other hand	~~Today~~

Introduction	Additional	Consequence
These days *Today*		

Conclusion	Contrast	Opinion

C Fill the gaps with a suitable expression. Use each expression only once.

The advantages and disadvantages of television

¹_____ it seems that we are watching more television than ever before, and doctors argue that we are getting lazier. ²_____ there is a great deal of debate at the moment about the advantages and disadvantages of television.

³_____ of television is its educational value. ⁴_____, many people learn about science by watching documentaries. ⁵_____, television provides company for people (the elderly, ⁶_____) who are unable to go out and meet friends.

⁷_____, television does have disadvantages. ⁸_____, it discourages people from taking exercise. Why go and play sport when you can sit on your sofa watching interesting programmes? ⁹_____, television discourages children from developing their imaginations. They can spend all day watching cartoons or playing computer games and ¹⁰_____ they do not invent their own games or play with other children.

¹¹_____, probably the best that we can do is to watch television sensibly. ¹²_____ all its disadvantages, there is no doubt that it is here to stay.

as a result
consequently
firstly
for example
for instance
in addition
in spite of
on the other hand
secondly
the main advantage
to sum up
today

Improve your speaking and writing

TOPIC notes

Use the TOPIC notes in Wordpower to improve your speaking and writing – fast!

A Read these questions from an English exam and think about your answers:
1 Do you have any pets?
2 Tell me about your home.
3 How important is music for you?
4 How do you spend your free time?
5 Do/did you enjoy life at school or university?
6 Tell me about the best holiday you've ever had.
7 Do you prefer travelling by bus, car, plane or train?
8 Would you rather be an artist, a secretary or a doctor?

B Now look at this list of some of the TOPIC notes in Wordpower. Which TOPIC notes can you use to answer the exam questions above? Write a number beside each topic. The first one has been done for you as an example:

art ___	jobs ___
books ___	listening to
bus ___	music ___
cars ___	literature ___
doctor ___	office work ___
dogs _1_	pets _1_
driving ___	plane ___
films ___	pop music ___
flat ___	schools ___
holidays ___	shopping ___
hospital ___	sport ___
hotel ___	studying ___
houses ___	television ___
humour ___	train ___
the Internet ___	university ___

Improve your speaking

Describing pictures:
In this picture there is .../you can see ...
He/She/It is/They are ...ing.
at the top/bottom
on the left/right

Speculating:
It looks like a .../It seems to be ...
It must/could/might/be ...

Comparing/Contrasting:
In this picture ..., whereas in that picture ...
This isn't as (attractive, interesting, etc.) a picture as that one, because ...
This picture reminds me of the time I (did/was/went to ..., etc.)
If I was/were in that situation, I'd ...

Expressing a preference:
I like ... more than ...
I'd (much) rather ... than ...
If I had to choose, I'd pick ...because ...

Giving your opinion:
In my opinion ...
Personally, I think that ...
It seems to me that ...

Asking for somebody's opinion
What do you think (about ...)?
What's your opinion?
How do you feel about ...?

Starting a discussion
Right, shall I start?
Would you like to start?
Shall we start with this picture?

Agreeing/Disagreeing:
Absolutely!
So do I./ I do too.
No, neither/nor do I.
I'm not sure about that.
Actually, I don't think that ...

Interrupting politely
Sorry to interrupt, but ...
Sorry, but I'd just like to make the point that ...
Could I just say that ...

Photocopiable © Oxford University Press

Formal and informal English

Informal English

Like idioms, many phrasal verbs and informal expressions have special meanings that are hard to understand, even if you know the meaning of the individual words. Match the **bold** words in the the text below with their meanings in the list (a–q):

These days, I'm so **broke** that I've had to move out of my flat. I'm £3,000 **in the red** and I had to find a way of **getting** my bank manager **off my back**. Still, **looking on the bright side**, at least I don't have to **fork out** much for rent now because a **mate** of mine is letting me stay at his **place** until things start to **look up**. The only thing is, he and his girlfriend are **going through a bad patch** and their rows are driving me **round the bend**. The last one was about where they should go on holiday. I mean, James is OK, but he's a bit of **a doormat** and **at the end of the day** Claire always **gets her own way**, so what's the point of him **digging his heels in** about where they go on holiday? I'm probably making the atmosphere worse by **playing gooseberry**, which must **be hard on** them. I suppose I should **get my act together** and find a job.

a overdrawn	h having problems	m gets what she wants
b mad	i pay	n organize myself
c poor	j stopping sb	properly
d a weak person	annoying me	o being with a couple
e improve	k the most important	when they want to be
f home	thing is	alone
g taking an	l refusing to change	p make things difficult for
optimistic view	his mind	q friend

Formal to informal

You can make your English more informal by replacing ordinary verbs with phrasal verbs that have the same meaning.

▸ *Example*: The fire fighters took four hours to **extinguish** the blaze.
I **put out** the fire with some water.

Replace the word in **bold** with a phrasal verb in the appropriate form. Use the word in brackets.

1 Shall we **continue** after lunch? (carry) *Shall we carry on after lunch?*
2 Tell the boss exactly what you think. Don't worry – I'll **support** you. (back)
3 You'll never guess who I **met** in the street just now! (bump)
4 I'm trying to **reduce** the amount of coffee I drink each day. (cut)
5 I'll have to **postpone** the meeting until next week. (put)
6 The flight is at 8.00 so we'll have to **leave** very early for the airport. (set)
7 I think the baby really **resembles** his mother. (take)
8 I was so pleased when my dad finally **stopped** smoking. (give)
9 It's amazing how some people manage to **raise** their children alone. (bring)
10 Have we got time to **visit** Elena on the way home? (drop)

Spelling

These words all have a silent consonant.

> **B** climb, comb, debt, doubt, dumb, lamb, thumb   **C** fascinating, muscle, science, yacht   **D** handkerchief, Wednesday   **G** champagne, foreign, sign
> **H** exhausted, honest, hour, yoghurt   **K** knee, knife, knob, knock, know   **L** calm, could, should, would, half, palm, salmon, talk, walk   **N** autumn   **P** psychiatrist, psychology, receipt   **R** iron   **S** island   **T** ballet, castle, duvet, fasten, listen, often, whistle   **W** answer, sword, who, whose, write, wrong

These words can be difficult to spell. The part of each word that usually causes problems is in **bold**.

acco**mm**odation	defi**nite**ly	o**pp**osite	reco**mm**end
add**r**ess	disa**pp**ointed	po**ss**e**ss**ion	sepa**r**ate
alright (but all right)	emba**rr**a**ss**ed	practi**se** (verb)	su**cc**e**ss**ful
	exa**gg**erate	practi**ce** (noun)	u**nn**ece**ss**ary
asso**c**iation	ex**c**ellent	(a TV)	until (but till)
ca**ss**ette	imm**ed**iately	programme	woo**ll**en
ciga**r**ette	indepen**d**ent	(US program)	
comm**er**cial	jewe**ll**ery	(a computer)	
comm**itt**ee	mille**nn**ium	program	

Here is one spelling rule that is worth learning! The sound /iː/ is often spelled **ie**, as in *piece* and *believe*. After the letter **c**, however, this is written **ei**, as in *receive*, *ceiling* and *receipt*. **Remember the rhyme**:

i before e except after c
(Two common exceptions are *seize* and *weird*.)

gh

In which of the words below

▸ is the gh silent?
▸ is the gh pronounced as /f/?
▸ is the gh pronounced as /g/?

ghetto	cough
night	although
ghost	daughter
higher	rough
enough	thorough
tough	

Double consonants

Some words double their final consonant when an ending such as –ing, –ed, –er, –able, etc is added, usually in order to show that the vowel that comes before is short. Fill the gaps in these sentences with the words on the left, doubling the final consonant where necessary.

fat	The baby's getting _____ er every day.
hope	I'm _____ ing to go to India next year.
stop	I _____ ed to look at the map.
write	I'm _____ ing to thank you for all your help.
write	Have you ever _____ en to a newspaper?
win	We've got no chance of _____ ing.
whine	The dog was _____ ing outside the door.
open	I cut my thumb while _____ ing a tin.
listen	You're not _____ ing to me!
plan	I had _____ ed to study but I fell asleep.
visit	Have you _____ ed him in hospital yet?
big	As usual, the boss got the _____ est pay rise.
refer	Whose mistake was he _____ ing to?
prefer	A boring job is _____ able to no job.
kidnap	The boy is believed to have been _____ ed.
beat	We were _____ en 4–0 in the final.

Photocopiable © Oxford University Press

Pronunciation

In English, the same letters (*for example,* ei) can be pronounced in several different ways:

receive	/rɪˈsiːv/	their	/ðeə/	height	/haɪt/
foreign	/ˈfɒrən/	weight	/weɪt/	leisure	/ˈleʒə/
weird	/wɪəd/				

The table below shows four vowel sounds that have various spellings. Put each word from the list into the correct column. For example, the pronunciation of moun<u>tain</u> is /ˈmaʊntɪn/, so you would write it in the ɪ column, and <u>other</u> is pronounced /ˈʌðə/ so you would write it in the ʌ column.

ə	ɪ	ʌ	ɜː
ago, father	sit	cup	turn
	mountain	*other*	

bird
bis<u>cuit</u>
blood
<u>bu</u>sy
cer<u>tain</u>
choco<u>late</u>
con<u>trol</u>
coun<u>try</u>
earth
ex<u>pert</u>
fam<u>ous</u>
heard
jou<u>rney</u>
language
mar<u>ried</u>
min<u>ute</u> (noun)

<u>money</u>
moun<u>tain</u> ✔
<u>mou</u>stache
nurse
one
or<u>ange</u>
other ✔
pack<u>age</u>
pack<u>et</u>
plea<u>sure</u>
pre<u>tty</u>
wo<u>man</u>
<u>wo</u>men
won
work

The sound ə is the most common vowel sound in English. It is pronounced softly, with the mouth relaxed and not forming any particular shape. ə only occurs in unstressed syllables.

Here are some more words that do not look like they sound. Fill the gaps with correct phonetic spelling.

beard	/b __ d/	iron	/ˈaɪ __ n/
beautiful	/ˈbjuː __ tɪfl/	naked	/ˈn __ k __ d/
break	/br __ k/	queue	/kj __ /
breakfast	/ˈbr __ kf __ st/	restaurant	/ˈrestr __ nt/
comfortable	/ˈk __ mft __ bl/	sausage	/ˈs __ s __ dʒ/
cupboard	/ˈk __ b __ d/	sew	/s __ /
friend	/fr __ nd/	stomach	/ˈst __ m __ k/
fruit	/fr __ t/	suit	/s __ t/
government	/ˈg __ vənm __ nt/	tired	/ˈtaɪ __ d/
guide	/g __ d/	vegetable	/ˈvedʒt __ bl/
heart	/h __ t/		

Photocopiable © Oxford University Press

Topic: Food and shopping

Going shopping

A shopping list

Here is a shopping list, but all the letters are jumbled up. Can you rearrange them?

~~nabansa~~ *bananas*
smoteato
dre preepp
stegcroute
clarig
midsekm likm
ecknich streabs
twieh newi

A shopping trip

Here is an account of a shopping trip. Use the words in the box to fill the gaps.

assistant groceries refund return special offers errand trolley sold out butcher's takeaway queue fit exchanged checkout receipt aisles

My first _____ was to go to the clothes shop, as I had to _____ a shirt I bought last week but which didn't _____ properly.

Unfortunately I didn't have the _____ , so the _____ told me I couldn't get a _____ .

Instead I _____ it for a shirt in a different style.

Next I went to the supermarket to buy _____ . I walked up and down the _____ , looking at this week's _____ and filling my _____ with all kinds of food. There was a _____ at the _____ , so I had to wait quite a long time. Next I went to the local _____ to buy some chicken for dinner. Unfortunately I was too late – they had _____ of chicken. I hope the family won't mind a _____ tonight!

Containers

Study the illustration at container in Wordpower. Then match the food with the appropriate container.

1	a bag of	chocolates
2	a bottle of	margarine
3	a box of	jam
4	a can of	toothpaste
5	a carton of	cola
6	a jar of	crisps
7	a tub of	water
8	a tube of	milk

What's cooking?

A Underline the words in the box that can be used as nouns **and** verbs.

blend boil chop defrost fry grill roast slice

B Now fill the gaps with some of the nouns from the box.

1 She put some butter on a _____ of toast.

2 Bring the water to the _____ before you put the spaghetti in.

3 This tea is a _____ of several types of leaf.

4 How many lamb _____ shall we cook for dinner?

Photocopiable © Oxford University Press

Topic: Clothes and appearance

Clothes and accessories

A Find 9 articles of clothing or accessories in the following box. Words can go across (➔) or down (↓). One word has been done for you as an example.

```
N H R E O K U E S O P
L Y K A M A S N W C U
G I D R I N L B I J O
E Q U R G M I R M Y S
R S A I A E P A S R W
O J P N X T P E U S E
F A T G O B E F I D A
S C U S C A R F T L T
P K D W A I S I (T I E)
H E L M E T L K O M R
L T C H P W B E L T V
```

B Now put the words you found into the sentences below. Use each word only once.

1 It is illegal to ride a motorcycle without a _____ .

2 Take those outdoor shoes off and put some _____ on.

3 My trousers are falling down! Can I borrow a _____ ?

4 We're not allowed to wear _____ or any other jewellery to school.

5 Aren't you cold in that T-shirt? Do you want to borrow a _____ ?

6 We have to dress quite formally for work – I am expected to wear a _____ and *tie* every day.

7 You need a nice woolly _____ to keep your neck warm on those cold winter mornings.

8 We're going to the beach later, so don't forget your _____ .

Talking about appearance

A One of the following is the correct way to ask for a description of a person's appearance. Which one?

1 How is she?
2 How is her look?
3 What does she look like?
4 What is she look like?

B Look at the rule in the box, then put the words and phrases in the appropriate columns:

> look + adjective
> look like + noun

She looks …	She looks like…

tired   you   a movie star
her mother   beautiful   happy

Which word?

Circle the word or phrase which is the most appropriate in each sentence.

1 You look/look like great – have you lost weight?

2 The colour of your tie doesn't fit/match your shirt.

3 That colour really fits/suits you.

4 How many items of clothing/clothes did you buy?

5 His jumper isn't big enough any more. It shrank/stretched in the wash.

6 Today I'm wearing/I wear jeans but I'm usually wearing/I usually wear a suit.

7 She's wearing/carrying glasses and wearing/carrying a bag.

8 My grandfather is in his mid-sixties/middle sixties.

Photocopiable © Oxford University Press

Topic: Sport

Types of sport

Put each sport into an appropriate box below. Some of them can go into more than one box.

aerobics	football	judo	soccer	volleyball
baseball	golf	running	swimming	weightlifting
basketball	gymnastics	skateboarding	table tennis	windsurfing
cricket	hockey	skiing	tennis	
fencing	ice skating	snowboarding	trampolining	

sports that you do outdoors	sports that you play with a ball	sports that you play with a bat, club, racket or stick	sports that you do indoors

sports that you play in a team	sports that you play with a net	sports that you do in cold weather	sports that you do in water

Sports words

Here are some useful words connected with sport. Match them with their definitions below.

coach	court	rink
match	referee	spectators
stadium		

1 an area where certain ball games such as basketball or tennis are played _____

2 a large structure, usually with no roof, where people can sit and watch sport

   _____

3 a person who controls a soccer game and prevents the rules from being broken _____

4 the people who are watching a sports event _____

5 an organized game of tennis

   _____

6 a person who trains people to compete in sports _____

7 a large area where people can skate or play ice hockey _____

Bat, club, racket or stick?

Fill the gaps with the correct words.

1 You play golf with a _____ .

2 You play hockey with a _____ .

3 You play baseball and cricket with a

   _____ .

4 You play tennis and badminton with a _____ .

Topic: Health

Useful words

Use the words in the box to fill the gaps in the sentences below. Use each word or phrase only once.

1 If you don't feel well, go and see your _____ .

2 When I cut my head, I needed eight _____ .

3 That looks like a serious injury. We'd better take him to _____ .

4 The _____ came into the room and took my temperature.

5 My doctor says I might need _____ on my knee.

6 I have an appointment to see a doctor at the local _____ .

7 My granny is recovering from a serious illness. She's a _____ at the Radcliffe Hospital.

8 Tom had tooth decay so the dentist gave him a _____ .

accident and
  emergency

clinic

filling

GP

nurse

patient

stitches

surgery

Giving advice

A Make sentences giving advice by matching a phrase on the left with a phrase on the right. In some cases more than one combination is possible.

1 You'd better ⟍   put some cream on it?
2 If I were you ⟋   sit down.
3 Why don't you   to put a plaster on it.
4 You ought   to get some rest.
5 You should   having a massage.
6 You could try   I'd go to the dentist.
7 Why don't you try   take a painkiller.
8 It would be a good idea   sucking a lozenge?

B Now write the number of a suitable piece of advice next to each problem.

I've got toothache. _____

I've got a splitting headache! _____

I'm coming down with the flu. _____

I've got a sore throat. _____

Ouch! I've twisted my ankle. _1_

I've got a huge mosquito bite. _____

I've cut my finger. _____

I'm suffering from stress. _____

Accidents and injuries

Label the illustration using the words in the box.

a bandage
a crutch
a plaster
a sling
plaster

Photocopiable © Oxford University Press

Topic: Where you live

City life or country life?

A Put the words into the correct column, according to whether they are usually associated with being in the city or with being in the countryside.

pollution	village	nature	field	peaceful
traffic	nightlife	skyscraper	hectic	rat race
remote	rush hour	suburbs	smog	cosmopolitan
picturesque				

City life	Country life

B Use some of the words from the columns above to complete the following paragraph about city life.

Many people believe that living in the city is better than living in the countryside. Of course, city life has its advantages. There are always plenty of things to do, and you need never be bored in a big city. However, city life is often _____, which can be stressful. _____ is also often a problem in cities, caused partly by the large amount of _____ on the roads. Most people live on the outskirts of cities, in the _____, and travelling to work every day during the _____ is also stressful.

C Now write a similar paragraph about country life.

Types of house

Look at colour page P5 of Wordpower. Which type of home does each of these people live in?

1 I live in a house that is arranged on only one storey. *bungalow*
2 My house is in a row of other similar houses that are all connected to each other.
3 I live on the 10th floor of a very high building.
4 I live in a small traditional house in a village in the countryside.
5 My house is connected on one side to another similar house, but not on the other side.
6 My house is not connected to another house on either side.

Photocopiable © Oxford University Press